Celebrations in My World

CHINESE
New Year

Crabtree Publishing Company

www.crabtreebooks.com

Crabtree Publishing Company

www.crabtreebooks.com

Author: Carrie Gleason
Coordinating editor: Chester Fisher
Series editor: Susan Labella
Project manager: Kavita Lad (Q2AMEDIA)
Art direction: Dibakar Acharjee (Q2AMEDIA)
Cover design: Tarang Saggar (Q2AMEDIA)
Design: Neha Sethi (Q2AMEDIA)
Photo research: Sakshi Saluja (Q2AMEDIA)
Editor: Kelley MacAulay
Copy editor: Adrianna Morganelli
Proofreader: Crystal Sikkens
Project editor: Robert Walker
Production coordinator: Katherine Berti
Font management: Mike Golka
Prepress technicians: Ken Wright

Photographs:
Cover: Steve Vidler/Photolibrary, McMac/Shutterstock (background); Title page: Cora Reed/Shutterstock; P4: Homestudiofoto/Dreamstime; P5: Keren Su/Getty Images; P6: Mary Evans Picture Library/Alamy; P7: Ben Heys/Shutterstock; P8: Mindy w.m. Chung/Shutterstock; P9: Lordprice Collection/Alamy; P10: Christine Gonsalves/Shutterstock; P11: Andrea Skjold/Dreamstime; P12: ZTS/Shutterstock; P13: Yao Sheng Bo/Dreamstime; P15: Reuters/Stringer Shanghai; P17: tomh1000/ Canstockphoto; P18: 2008 China Photos/Getty Images; P19: Tamara Kulikova/Shutterstock; P21: Keellla/ Shutterstock; P22: OTHK/Getty Images; P23: Design56/ Dreamstime; P24: Keren Su/Getty Images; P25: Ginaellen/ Dreamstime; P26: nao/Stockxpert; P27: Reuters/Claro Cortes; P28: Foong Kok Leong/Shutterstock; P29: Billy Hustace/Getty Images; P30: John Leung/Shutterstock; P31: Ambient Images Inc./Alamy

Library and Archives Canada Cataloguing in Publication

Gleason, Carrie, 1973-
    Chinese New Year / Carrie Gleason.

(Celebrations in my world)
Includes index.

ISBN 978-0-7787-4280-7 (bound).--ISBN 978-0-7787-4298-2 (pbk.)

    1. Chinese New Year--Juvenile literature. I. Title. II. Series.

GT4905.G54 2008   j394.261   C2008-903488-0

Library of Congress Cataloging-in-Publication Data

Gleason, Carrie, 1973-
    Chinese new year / Carrie Gleason.
        p. cm. -- (Celebrations in my world)
    Includes index.
    ISBN-13: 978-0-7787-4298-2 (pbk. : alk. paper)
    ISBN-10: 0-7787-4298-9 (pbk. : alk. paper)
    ISBN-13: 978-0-7787-4280-7 (reinforced library binding : alk. paper)
    ISBN-10: 0-7787-4280-6 (reinforced library binding : alk. paper)
    1. Chinese New Year--Juvenile literature. 2. China--Social life and customs--Juvenile literature. I. Title. II. Series.

GT4905.G54 2009
394.261--dc22
                                          2008023529

Crabtree Publishing Company

Printed in China/082011/FC20110523

www.crabtreebooks.com   1-800-387-7650

Published in Canada
Crabtree Publishing
616 Welland Ave.
St. Catharines, Ontario
L2M 5V6

Published in the United States
Crabtree Publishing
PMB 59051
350 Fifth Avenue, 59th Floor
New York, New York 10118

Published in the United Kingdom
Crabtree Publishing
Maritime House
Basin Road North, Hove
BN41 1WR

Published in Australia
Crabtree Publishing
386 Mt. Alexander Rd.
Ascot Vale (Melbourne)
VIC 3032

Contents

Lucky New Year

Everywhere in China fireworks explode and long paper dragons wind through the streets. It is time for the Chinese New Year celebration!

Chinese New Year welcomes the start of a new year. It is the most important celebration in China. People enjoy this holiday in many different ways.

● Two **symbols** of good luck during Chinese New Year are peaches and the color red. Firecrackers are set off to scare away bad luck.

DID YOU KNOW?

*Chinese people follow certain **traditions** to make sure they have a lucky new year.*

Chinese New Year "dragons" are made from **papier-mâché**, paper, silk, and bamboo sticks. Dancers control the dragon's snake-like body.

Spirits and Gods

Long ago, ancient Chinese farmers planted their rice crops in spring. While they waited for the plants to grow, they cleaned their homes and prayed for a good harvest. Over thousands of years, this time spent waiting developed into the Chinese New Year celebration. Many ancient customs are still a part of Chinese New Year today.

● Taoism is a Chinese religion. One of the most important Taoist gods is the Jade Emperor, who rules over heaven.

DID YOU KNOW?

*The ancient Chinese believed that spirits of their dead **ancestors** watched over them. They made offerings to the ancestors so they would receive good blessings.*

Today, many Chinese people practice a religion called Buddhism. They follow the teaching of the Buddha and visit temples during New Year celebrations.

The ancient Chinese believed in many gods and spirits. The spirits could be good or evil. To scare away evil spirits, people lit bonfires or set off fireworks. Today, this tradition continues during Chinese New Year.

The Kitchen God

One of the most important gods of the Chinese New Year is the Kitchen God. All year long, a picture of the Kitchen God hangs in family kitchens. A week before the new year, families set up a kitchen altar. **Incense** and sticky, sweet cakes are put on the altar as offerings to the Kitchen God. Then, the picture of the Kitchen God is burned. This symbolizes the Kitchen God going to Heaven, where he reports to the Jade Emperor on the families.

DID YOU KNOW?

These sticky sweet cakes are called niango *(shown above). Nian* means "year."

Chinese people hope the cakes will "sweeten" the report he gives to the Jade Emperor, bringing them happiness in the coming year. Others hope the sticky treats will make the Kitchen God's mouth stick shut so he cannot give a report at all!

This picture shows the Kitchen God. Once the Kitchen God has left, the preparations for Chinese New Year begin!

Getting Ready

There are many things to buy for the New Year celebration. Children may receive puppets as a special treat.

Some people think that using sharp tools such as knives or scissors at the beginning of the new year can "cut off" good luck.

There is a lot to do to prepare for Chinese New Year. People believe it is bad luck to clean or cook food during the first five days of the new year, so everything is done before the year ends.

People take special care when cleaning their homes for the celebration. Cleaning rids the home of all the previous year's bad luck and makes room for good luck in the coming year. Some people also go to graveyards to clean the graves of their ancestors.

● All the food that will be eaten during the Chinese New Year celebration, such as these dumplings, is prepared in advance.

Years ago, people took baths with mint leaves in the water on New Year's Eve, believing this would make them extra clean. They thought that washing on New Year's Day would "wash away" their good luck. Today, many people get their hair cut and buy new clothes before New Year's Day. They usually buy red clothes because the color red stands for happiness. Some people hope that by changing their appearance with new clothes and a haircut, evil spirits from the year before will not know who they are.

DID YOU KNOW?

Chinese New Year is also called the Spring Festival. In the past, plum blossoms (shown at left) were hung over doorways. These blossoms come in spring.

People hang long red banners with good luck wishes written on them around their homes.

Before the new year, people also pay back any money they owe and settle disagreements with their families and friends. Children catch up on schoolwork and adults make sure their work is done. Everything must be perfect for New Year's Day so that the coming year will be full of good things.

New Year's Eve

People travel from all over China to be with their families on New Year's Eve. Another household member also returns on New Year's Eve—the Kitchen God! The family hangs a new picture of him in the kitchen. People stay up very late on New Year's Eve, feasting and visiting with family. At midnight, fireworks explode in the sky. People also set off firecrackers. These bright lights and loud noises are believed to scare away the old year and evil spirits.

DID YOU KNOW?

Firecrackers were once made from bamboo stems. The burning hollow stems make a loud sound as they split open.

14

In this community in Southwest China, everyone eats together on New Year's Eve at a table that seats 1,000 people!

Food and Feasts

Having all the family together for the New Year's Eve feast is like having a **reunion**. At the feast, people eat round foods, such as dumplings. To make dumplings, dough is stuffed with seasoned meat, fish, and cabbage, then it is boiled or fried. Sometimes, coins are hidden inside. Whoever gets a dumpling with a coin will have wealth in the new year. Meat and vegetable dishes are also served.

DID YOU KNOW?

Meat, such as chicken, turkey, or duck, is served whole to symbolize good luck for the whole year.

Long noodles are eaten. Some people think that cutting the noodles means cutting life short. For dessert, people eat *niango*.

For family and friends, trays of snacks are set out. Each food in the tray has a special meaning. Women wishing to have many children should eat the lotus seeds.

Chinese Calendar

Chinese New Year's Day falls sometime in January or February each year. The Chinese calendar that keeps track of festival dates is based on the **lunar** calendar. Lunar means "moon." The lunar calendar follows the cycles of the Moon.

● This boy is all dressed up and ready for a Chinese New Year's party.

DID YOU KNOW?

Fish are a symbol of plenty. The Chinese symbol for fish and plenty are the same.

18

Chinese New Year begins on the first New Moon of the lunar calendar. During this time, the Moon cannot be seen in the night sky. Chinese New Year ends 15 days later, during the first Full Moon of the year.

This chart shows some of the phases of the Moon.

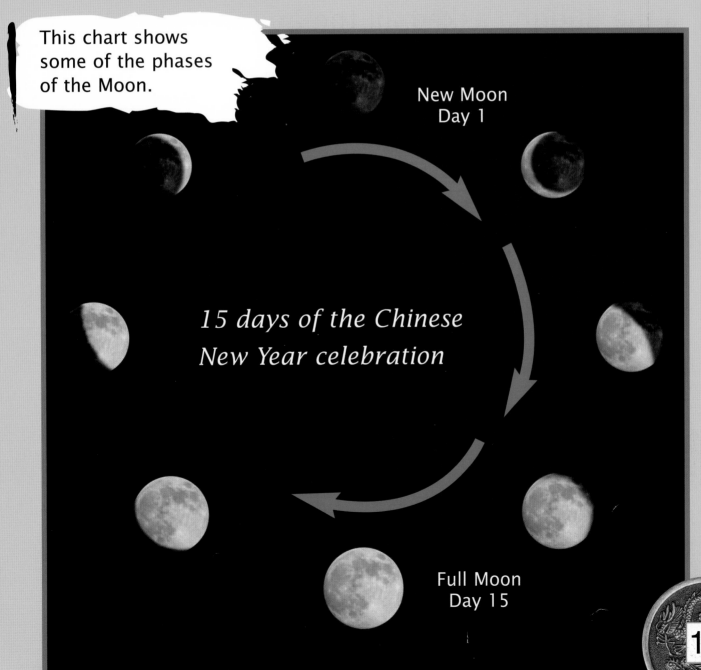

New Moon
Day 1

15 days of the Chinese New Year celebration

Full Moon
Day 15

Year of the. . .

Each new year is ruled by one of the 12 animals of the Chinese **zodiac**. According to one legend, the animals were chosen by the Buddha. One day the Buddha asked all the animals to come and visit him. The animals that showed up are pictured on page 21. Over time, it was believed that people took on the **traits** of the animal that ruled the year they were born. Which one of these animals do you think you are most like? Match the year of your birth to the animal of the zodiac.

DID YOU KNOW?

Some people believe the animals of the zodiac were chosen by the Jade Emperor. He called all the animals to take part in a contest. The rat was the winner!

2008 – Rat: You are charming, **ambitious**, and you like adventure.

2002 – Horse: You are popular, cheerful, and do well in sports.

2009 – Ox: You are patient, strong, and a natural leader.

2003 – Sheep: You are calm, creative, and you care a lot about others.

1998 – Tiger: You are caring, **sensitive**, and filled with courage.

2004 – Monkey: You are smart, polite, and funny.

1999 – Rabbit: You are lucky, loving, and careful in all that you do.

2005 – Rooster: You are honest, hardworking, and clever.

2000– Dragon: You are honest, brave, and have a lot of energy.

2006 – Dog: You are generous, brave, and **dependable**.

2001– Snake: You are wise, quiet, and charming.

2007 – Pig: You are honest, giving, and kind.

Welcome New Year!

People set off fireworks to welcome the new year.

On New Year's Day, people throw open their doors and windows to let in the new year. People greet each other with wishes of "Happy New Year!" In Chinese they say "*Sun Nien Fai Lok!*" or "*Xin Nian Kuai Le!*"

DID YOU KNOW?

Pictures of two door gods are hung in doorways. The door gods are believed to keep evil spirits from entering the house.

The first words someone says on New Year's Day sets the tone for the whole year. Throughout the day, people are careful not to argue, and children are not scolded. Only good things are spoken on this day. A popular greeting to someone you meet is "*Gung Hay Fat Choy,*" which means "Wishing you happiness and wealth." People are careful not to cry on New Year's Day, or they may end up crying all year long!

Most people spend New Year's Day visiting friends and family. They bring gifts of flowers and fruit. Children receive red envelopes called *hongbao* or *lai shi*. Inside the envelopes is lucky money!

● Children receive money in red envelopes as gifts.

After spending time with family, large crowds gather together to celebrate the new year.

Children show respect to their elders during Chinese New Year. They must wait until their elders have eaten before beginning their own meals. Children bow to their elders, and bring them tea in the morning. During the holiday, many families visit temples, where they pray to their ancestors and other spirits for good fortune.

After the first three to five days of celebrating, stores reopen and most people's lives return to normal. In some ways, however, the celebration continues for the next ten days.

People light sticks of incense at temples. These are called joss sticks.

DID YOU KNOW?

Many Chinese people do not celebrate their birthday on the anniversary of the day they were born. Instead, they celebrate their birthday during Chinese New Year.

Sights and Sounds

Lively parades filled with colorful costumes, dancing, and the sounds of drums and **gongs** take place all through Chinese New Year. Dragon dances are performed all over China. At the front of the dragon, a dancer holds up the huge head. More dancers follow behind with the body. Lion dances feature a puppet with a giant lion's head. Lion dances are believed to chase off evil and to bring good luck to shopkeepers.

DID YOU KNOW?

Dragons are also a symbol of spring in China. According to one legend, people began performing dragon dances to wake up a dragon that brought spring rain for newly planted crops.

Some even have pieces of paper hanging from them with riddles written on them. Everyone has a good time trying to figure out the answers to the riddles.

Large displays of lights include many kinds of shapes and figures.

Chinese Abroad

Chinese New Year is celebrated by over a billion people around the world. Over time, many Chinese people left China and settled in other countries. Wherever large groups of Chinese people live, Chinese New Year is celebrated.

These girls in the United States are dressed for a Chinese New Year parade.

DID YOU KNOW?

*Chinese New Year is a holiday in many **Southeast Asian** countries.*

In the United States, Canada, and England, large cities have areas called Chinatowns where Chinese culture thrives. In each of these countries, Chinese New Year is celebrated differently, but most feature a parade and a dragon dance. Chinese New Year is not an official holiday in these countries, as it is in China, so most people celebrate after work or school. New Year's dinner is an important part of the celebration.

A Chinese marching band playing traditional drums takes part in a Chinese New Year parade through New York City's Chinatown.

Glossary

ambitious Eager for success

ancestor Someone from whom one is descended; a relative from way back

dependable Someone you can rely on

gong A large metal cymbal

incense Something that gives off a pleasing smell when burned

lunar Moon

papier-mâché A workable mixture of paper and glue that becomes hard with it dries

reunion A gathering of people who haven't seen one another in a while

sensitive Having feelings that are easily hurt

Southeast Asia The countries that lie between India, China, and Australia on a map

symbol An image, word, or object that stands for something else

tradition Something that has been done over and over again for a long time

traits The way you are

zodiac The twelve sections of the sky as divided by astrologers. Each section is represented by an animal

Index